GW01395814

De
to
the
helpful tool as
you raise destinie

I'm Telling!

What Every Mother Should Tell her Daughter

with love
from auntie
Verna
xx.
27/12/13

Sonya Lowe

Foreword by Payton Corryn Lowe

For Avery & Payton

This Book is dedicated to my mother, Tommie Young...

❧

The hardest role is that of mother; not to mention the mother that is dedicated & invested in the future of her children. For your prayers, commitment & encouragement "I am" so graciously I say "Thank you"

Acknowledgements

I want to personally thank all of you for your continuous support but unfortunately, I am only allowed a certain amount of space to salute the many people who make it all possible for me. First and foremost, thank the Lord for blessing my thoughts and directing my path so that I can actually touch hearts and lives in a positive way. It's my prayer that anyone picking up this book will be blessed by something within the pages. A very special thanks to my daughters, Avery and Payton, I am very proud of you both; you're my best work ever and I love you. My attorney and good friend Robbie ~ I am forever in your debt. An extra special thanks to Downey Simple Pleasures and Barnes & Noble Bookstores worldwide for continuing to display love and support for what I do. M.A.D.E. Women for uplifting and giving power to a new generation of women! I am thankful for everyone else who has had the courage to believe wholeheartedly in things unseen; especially all the mothers out there that have faith in the big dreams of their daughters. For me, everything is possible through my Lord and Savior ~ Jesus Christ.

Sincerely...

Sonya

I'M TELLING!

Forward

Have you ever thought about what life would be like without your mother? Well I can't even imagine my life without my mom. I spend everyday of my life with her and when we're not together I miss her so much. All the fun times I have with her makes me regret times when I have been selfish. Whenever I say 'things are unfair' and 'why does she always do that' I quickly remember that she only wants what's best for me so there must be good reason. From my mother's wisdom, I can honestly decipher the right and wrong way to approach my own life.

I have watched my mother at her laptop as long as I can remember writing her articles, researching various topics, or writing scripts or books. It was clear at a very early age that my mother's passion is simply writing. She has that undying thirst for knowledge and the mission to empower other women by writing books, speaking to packed houses and placing articles with online magazines that keep women inspired. She has only exemplified strength, courage and elegance to me and my sister. I am so honored to offer my mother's book to you. This book is an enthusiastic celebration of my mommy's dedication to provide a blueprint for all mothers to establish a healthy, respectful relationship with their daughters.

I am very proud of my mommy and I am confident that this book will encourage every mother and daughter to evaluate their relationships. I do hope that you will find this book entertaining and enlightening at the same time. Thank you for sharing in my mommy's dream.

With love,
Payton Corryn Lowe

Dialogue is Important

This may sound silly but I'm still waiting for the talk. Yes, "the talk". I can honestly say, after a couple of serious relationships, a marriage, two kids, and a divorce, I am ready to finally have that dreaded talk with my mother. I'm not embarrassed to say that it's about thirty-five years overdue, but better late than never, right?

I'm from that era where we were told to "just say no!" to everything related to the male species and we would be fine. You may chuckle but this is the truth (and for the record my sister, who is ten years older than me, didn't get "the talk" either). However, there were some things that could have been addressed in my early teens that would have alleviated some of the mistakes along the way. Although my mistakes were minor in contrast to some of the girls in my neighborhood, they still were mistakes nonetheless.

As mothers, we have to understand that our daughters will often figure we are out of touch with what's really going on in the world today. We have to sincerely forgive them for being naïve and not grasping the concept that we have been there and done that. Realistically, we can all remember that day when we just knew that our mothers were some foreign being from outer space or worse ~ the fifties! Today, I can truly say I am thankful for my old fashion upbringing and the strict rules and guidelines that my parents set forth. Without their unwavering guidance and continuous demand for bigger and better, I don't know where I would have ended up. With that said I would never blame them or point the finger at my parents for things that I felt should have been different.

Having two daughters of my own and having them go from four to fourteen in what seems like overnight, recently I had to decide if I was going to let them learn the hard lessons themselves with their friends who are just as confused as they are or if I would take on the responsibility of at least equipping them with some knowledge that could help. I really had no choice in the matter. What was I suppose to do let my daughter get her knowledge from one of her little teenage girlfriends or ~ tell her the absolute truth? Although the first choice could have been the most comfortable for me, I chose the later. You should have seen the look on her face!

The most important thing for me is to let my daughters know that I'm willing to discuss anything that peaks their curiosity. I know as they continue to grow and experience more of life, they will have more questions that may be a little embarrassing for me but I will devote my attention to making sure that they're equipped with information that will help them make sound decisions and hopefully – by the grace of God – steer them away from some of the very pitfalls that all women reflect on in hindsight.

In an effort to make sure that my daughters don't make the same mistakes that I have made, I promised myself (and them) that I would always avail myself to their concerns and be a listening ear ~ even if I don't necessarily agree with what I'm hearing. Right now, at fifteen and sixteen, I must say that the concerns are minor but the questions are getting tougher and more difficult to answer. One thing I found to be true was that in order to be honest with my daughters, I had to first be honest with myself and admit that I too have had areas of insecurities throughout my life and that maybe I too have suffered from esteem issues at different periods in my life. I had to also face some of my fears that come along with being a single Black woman with two teenage daughters in this day and time; a single Black mother who is sacrificing her own happiness for theirs (and I would do it all again).

As women, we have been tasked to lead our daughters safely into womanhood with values and morals ~ and most importantly the knowledge ~ that will only create wonderfully amazing women. Let us not forget that they mimic what they see. This has been proven time and time again in modern day society. If your daughter sees you in relationships that are reckless and destructive, she will only learn that these relationships are acceptable because they were good enough for you. I know I only wish the very best for my daughters and so the theory of them accepting abusive, violent relationships is unthinkable for me. In addition, I want so badly to help them not become victims to various schemes and games that men play in the world we live in. With experience comes knowledge and wisdom; the knowledge and wisdom that we collectively need to share with young women who will otherwise make the same mistakes that their mothers and their mother's mothers have made but the difference is they may not be as lucky as we all have been. The rules have changed drastically and the games have become deadly ~ how will they survive them without the insight of their mothers?

This book pays homage to all the mothers out there who have been a force in their children's lives ~ being a mother is one of the most supreme duties and I'm telling you what has worked for me; the pages of this book contain simple suggestions to help you start talking to your daughter in a language she can understand and is intended to be the blueprint to building healthy, respectful relationships between mothers and daughters.

Use the space below to generate a list of topics that are of immediate concern to you; note things that you absolutely pray she never has to endure. Write what you want for your daughter's future and how you can assist her to achieve her goals (use additional paper if necessary). Be aware that raising upstanding, powerful young women is a task that shouldn't be taken lightly and we owe it to our daughters to invest in their well-being. If they owe us success, we certainly owe them commitment.

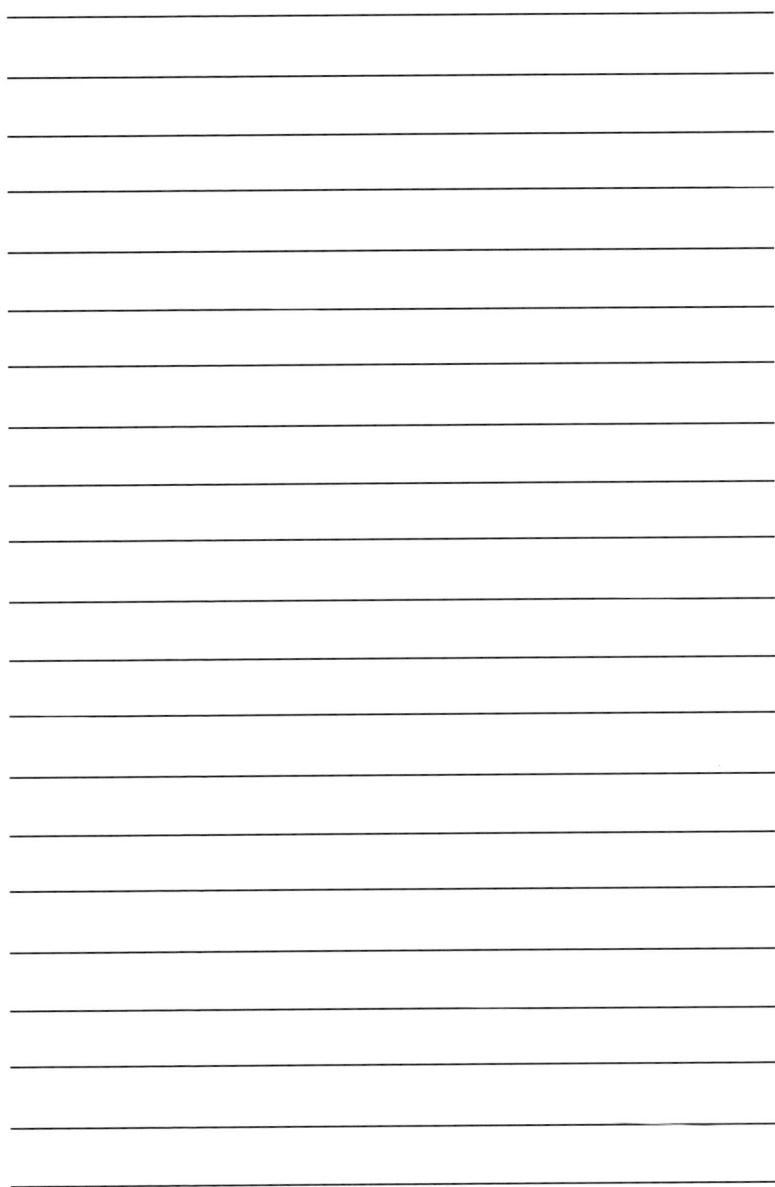

Be sure that you make time, at some point, to sit down with your daughter and discuss her objectives and goals in detail. You may also want to share this page of the book with her to allow insight into what your heart desires for her. Most of all you have to make certain to allow her room to be her own person, allow her to set her own objectives and goals, and most importantly, to not be judgmental if her views do not completely resemble yours.

Although we can not shelter their tender hearts from every ounce of pain, we can certainly share with them the gifts of knowledge, experience and unconditional love that will help them grow. In the following pages are just a few points that we should make sure to tell them because they need to know...

Tell Her She Has Power…

The thing women have yet to learn is nobody gives you power. You just take it.
Roseanne Barr

I can still remember the day I realized that I had power. As a young Black woman, I was powerful! It was on that day, that although I would encounter many obstacles, I realized that I could not and would not be defeated. Of course, since then, my setbacks have been plenty; certainly more than a few but that moment when I discovered who "I really was" I knew that I could do anything I truly wanted to do. Any and everything was in reach because I possessed an undying power. With hard work and dedication, I could truly live a life abundantly filled with joy, love and success. It took me a while to get to this frame of mind because I had to decide that I wanted to be better than what society had planned for me and I wanted to have a voice that would impact women all over the world. Moreover, I had to really accept the fact that I *deserved* everything that was great. Why wouldn't I deserve the very best?

Our daughters are faced with many challenges; many of which can make them feel unworthy and unvalued. With the way that media depicts women, and especially women of color, we have to let our daughters know that being a woman is a great gift in itself and although we may face negative imagery; we can also rise above those things that tend to corrupt our thoughts about ourselves and our worth. It is vital that we share with our teenage daughters that they can be different and be accepted. Its okay to march to the beat of a different drum ~ her own ~ and take control of her own journey. She needs to know that she is not the first to be challenged with the task of finding her own beauty and igniting her own spirit.

As a single parent of two teenage daughters (ages fifteen and sixteen at the time of the publishing of this book), I'm telling you that we have squared off on issues that my parents would have never even considered negotiating. With me being from that era where children were seen and not heard, my daughters' voicing their opinions is an idea I had to get use to. *Really*. What was considered talking back in my day is now considered freedom of expression and for the most part it serves as an outlet for our daughters to be upfront and honest with us about who they are and what they want.

It is vital that our daughters know their individual value and the power that comes along with it. This may sound a little old fashion and somewhat conservative but the fact is, most of the old school values that our mothers tried so hard to bestow upon us, certainly needs to be passed on to our daughters. I say this because of the media and the influence that it has on today's youth. I know some of the images I see on television have made me second guess what we represent. As we grow as women, we all recognize at some point that it is best to ignite your energy and power by first believing that there is the existence of something larger than our being. My power comes from the mere fact that I let the spirit work through me and the things I do. Although economics play a huge role in imagery, we have the power to overcome anything that is planted in our lives to cripple and distract us from that which is our purpose and plan. Our image of ourselves far exceeds any image the media can paint.

So I say it is important that we make sure our daughters are aware of the true power that comes with being a determined, driven, young woman. Not to compare our daughters to the women of Hollywood but I'm telling you that we have to be prepared to point out that which is authentic from that which is truly phony for the most part. It is our responsibility to make sure that they are aware of the beauty that they possess just with being their own person and not being drawn into those things that cheapen her image and elegance. I am the first to say that the media and the images that clutter our society are embarrassing and degrading of women and especially in depicting women of color so it is vital for us, as mothers, to make sure that we convey those ideas and thoughts that allow our daughters to see their worth in a society that doesn't always value who we are or what we experience. They have to know that they are very valuable components in the scheme of things.

Understand that by acknowledging our power doesn't lessen us as women but empowers us further to strive to meet the challenges that we will ultimately face, without a doubt, along this journey. Everyone is strengthened by a powerful woman; a strong woman of conviction and morals. All great men recognized the beauty of a woman possessing power. But enough with power; I think you get the picture...

Tell Her to Know Herself...

"One of the lessons that I grew up with was to always stay true to yourself and never let what somebody else says distract you from your goals. And so when I hear about negative and false attacks, I really don't invest any energy in them, because I know who I am".
First Lady, Michelle Obama

Everyone that knows me personally has asked me why I always jot notes to myself. I have pondered the answer for years. I believe that realistically while attending California State University, Long Beach, where I majored in Journalism, it became a habit to always write down those things that may have danced in my head or even points I would use in articles for the school newspaper. Nonetheless, the habit stuck with me. So if you should see me out and about around Los Angeles, don't be alarmed if I'm jotting thoughts in a purse size notebook. This is just who I am. I accept myself as I am and I determine those things that I may need to change. No one defines me or my existence; I have been spiritually empowered to take control of my own destiny. I would rather be myself everyday of the week, instead of pretending to be someone else just one day out of the week. I have a true testimony about loving myself ~ I love my eyes even with my glasses on, I love every curve on my body, I love everything about me that separates me from you. However, I am intelligent enough to know that there is always room for improvement. Funny thing about self-love is that when we learn to love ourselves, we attract those people who can appreciate and reciprocate that love.

Let's first say that if it is true that we teach people how to treat us, then we should always be treating ourselves like queens, wouldn't you agree? Let me give you an example: I met a woman who said her husband only wore the best designer clothes and shoes but when it came to her, he thought she would be okay shopping in discount stores. So when her birthday rolled around she was given a gift from a local outlet store. She was so upset that she asked him why he believed it was acceptable that he get her a "cheap" gift for her birthday when she had gone out of her way for on his birthday. His response was an eye opener. He said he likes nice things so she was just getting him a gift that would be up to his standards and he got her a cheap gift because she loves bargains so he thought she would be happy to know he got her a great gift and caught it on clearance in an outlet store. Trust me, this is a true story. We all know it is the thought that counts but he innocently believed that his wife would really be elated that he got a good price on a somewhat nice gift. Through this dialogue, you can ascertain that the wife has taught her husband that to her a bargain is everything. He has shown her that he feels he is worth finer things and would be enraged if she would have bought his birthday gift from a factory outlet store.

I referenced this scenario so that you have a visual of how ~ not just men but everyone around us ~ determine the best way to treat us. My advice would be lead by example and don't expect anyone to treat you better than you treat yourself. Once we get out of the mindset that our mates should honor us with flowers, diamonds, etc. and we start honoring ourselves on a daily basis, the results will be surprising. I can remember the first time I bought myself roses after thinking that the man in my life would finally "get it". *Instead I got it!* How empowering it was! It has been about thirteen years and I still buy myself roses on a weekly basis; it's a routine. Buy my own jewelry too. Funny, the man in my life now says 'what do you buy a woman who can buy herself the best gifts?' Most importantly, I realized how deserving I am ~ I work hard each day and yes I should buy myself flowers. For you it may be something else but I'm telling you now you deserve it. Never short change yourself...

  It is up to us to tell our daughters they deserve everything that is great; thus letting them know that they are worthy of the absolute best in everything. This is even more important if you are, like I am, a single mother with no father around on a full time basis. Fortunately, my daughters' father is very involved and tries his hardest to be a great father without my involvement.   But at the same time, it is my responsibility to make sure my daughters know that have the ability to move mountains if they want to. See I have twenty-four hour access to them and can make a huge difference if I approach it correctly. Moreover, it is a daily ritual for me to tell my children that they are powerful and the world belongs to them. I also believe that by telling my daughters that I love them dearly reinforces their confidence in "who" they really are and who they are expected to become. Let's face it, positive affirmations will go a long way when they start to make crucial decisions. Try it for yourself and see the difference in your daughter. I guarantee that you will see positive changes in your daughter once you put this strategy into practice.

And in the meantime, be good to yourself and tell your daughter to do the same.

Tell Her to Be a Friend...

To have loyal friends: you have to first be a loyal friend yourself.
Sincerely Sonya

When I was in my late teens, so-called friends would come and go so quick that it would make your head spin. At that time in my life it was all about having fun, hanging out, making sure there wasn't a strand of hair out of place, and that I was rocking the latest outfits, of course. I never really looked deep into who my friends were because frankly they didn't even know and I didn't really care as long as they appeared to be solid people from my point of view. My motto was certainly live and let live!

And then I grew up... The first thing I realized was that I had not been the best friend that I could be; had told secrets that probably were better off untold and maybe had spent time with a person or two that I really didn't like for whatever reason. When I recognized my destructive behavior, I was then left with the question of how many people had done the same thing in regards to me and being my friend. It was that moment that I realized that in order to have loyal friends; you have to first be a loyal friend yourself. People take the friendship role so lightly these days and have little respect for lifetime relationships but as women we have to develop those relationships and work hard at being a good friend just like we do at being a good lover, mother, wife, girlfriend, employee, etc.

In honor of the sisterhood that we must maintain among one another, we first need to make positive to establish the rules of engagement with our friends. At the top of my list for my sister friends is please don't talk to, date, call, etc. my ex-husband, ex-boyfriend, ex-whatever, after I have severed ties. That's just not cool and always leads to chaos. Seriously speaking, what would my "ex" have in common with my sister friends other than me?

For me the secret recipe to a great friendship is first being loyal; by providing me the exact same support in any given situation that I have provided to them.

And even when times are strained with our given careers, families, school and whatever else we partake, understand that lack of communication doesn't mean lack of love, respect or friendship. One of my good friends, who has known me every since the birth of my first daughter (and pregnant with the second one), took me out to brunch recently and said that no matter how much time elapse between our getting together or speaking on the phone, we always pick up where we left off. We all will face our own unique situations and circumstances, so time apart is almost guaranteed which leads us to what is important; the time we have together.

My childhood friend (we met in third grade) and I always kept in touch. Even after her mother and stepfather divorced and she and her family moved to the suburbia Southern California (forty-five minutes outside of Los Angeles), we remained friends. Although we weren't in constant contact, we managed to talk frequently about our lives, boyfriends, disappointments and blessings. So imagine how I felt when during planning my wedding, we disagreed and cut off all communications. It just would have been more fitting for her to support me as I had done for her on so many occasions rather than to give me her opinion at one of the happiest times in my life. My attitude was "if she can't support me, why would I need to include her?"

Fast forward ten years later, when I was then going through my divorce and my life spinning out of control ~ I saw a ghost! It was her younger sister who was then all grown up and working under my supervision at a remote location. When I saw her I knew exactly who she was and quickly asked her about my friend. She had such a puzzled look on her face and asked if there was somewhere we could talk privately. The news she gave me broke my heart. Why had I waited so long to contact my friend? And more importantly why hadn't I turned the other cheek when she gave her opinion?

And although I had so many times wondered why she hadn't called, my pride wouldn't let me look for her. Then there was several occurrences where I had called the last known number, asked for her and the woman on the other end would simply hang up. It all made sense after her sister told me that she had been murdered by her boyfriend a month before my wedding. You could never imagine the pain I felt and how sorry I was that I had allowed our separation to last so long. The pain and sorrow was beyond measure... I must say it broke my heart and made me more mature in my dealings with my sister friends. I am a friend and a damn good one these days!

So from that experience, I'm telling you that you have to make sure that stupid, childish things don't make you lose someone you love ~ on any level! What this experience required me to do was definitely grow up and grow into those things I always proclaimed to be. Some won't understand but it is a fact that sometimes we say we're all these wonderful things until we're put to the actual test. If you can't stand and deliver when it counts, then you have not passed the test. Of course, I should have handled the situation differently. When you reflect back on the type of friend you have been to someone and how they have perceived your actions, all you have to do is put yourself in there shoes.

I am qualified to say what you should do because I have been the worse friend ever and now relish in the rewards of being a true, loyal friend and only attracting the same. So make sure you tell your daughter to be a good friend and expect it in return. Tell her that being a good friend means being responsible enough to want the best for her friends and seeing past her pride to make the friendship work. Tell her to pray that her friends are blessed with an abundance of love, joy and happiness. And lastly, make sure you're providing her with behavior that exemplifies the same. I am a good (Great!) friend and I am surrounded by loyal men and women that I consider great friends as well. I am now very selective in whom I share myself, my time and my life with ~ I encourage my daughters to do the same...

Tell Her to Be Responsible...

"I don't think of myself as a poor deprived ghetto girl who made good. I think of myself as somebody who from an early age knew I was responsible for myself, and I had to make good."
Oprah

For everything ~ good and bad ~ in our lives we must be accountable. There's more to be said for taking responsibility for ones self than what we will ever imagine. I can recall many friends that would blame their parents for their short comings (or more like their bad decisions) so early in my life I decided to take responsibility for myself. Who could own up to my errors other than myself? You see, my parents weren't the type to make excuses for their kids anyway so blaming them would be useless. Luckily for me my parents always encouraged me to make my own decisions and live with them. You would have to imagine at the time that I thought they were just being tough; AGAIN!

My parents taught me the grim reality that everyone wasn't going to celebrate my victories with me, that some would rather see me do bad, and that I could either prove them right or wrong. I think it was this reality that made me start to really take ownership of my actions, deeds, and ultimately my life. Our daughters will have to face this reality a lot sooner than I did because the world has changed tremendously. In addition, responsibility covers a lot of territory. I mean it's more than taking on the day to day task of everyday life; it means to be accountable in all areas of your life.

I'm telling you that if we teach our daughters to be responsible when they're young, they will eagerly practice this behavior when they're older. We cannot require them to take on the task of being responsible and accountable if we have not told them what is expected.

A huge part of being responsible for me is to be a woman of my word and respecting the next person enough to let them know when I won't be able to honor my word.

We all know that person who tells us they're going to do something but won't answer their phone when we call them. If you're like me, you can easily determine that they're undependable and shouldn't be taken to heart. They're actions support this opinion, don't you agree?

It is my opinion that parenting is to be taken seriously and sometimes that will involve taking on hard duties to make sure our daughters are equipped with the tools to make sound judgment. We owe them everything we have to help them be all they can be. So again, it is not about punishing our daughters for behavior that may not be in line with what we personally would rather see but instead helping her to take full responsibility for herself and encourage accountability to herself ~ making her more focused on who she is and where she's headed.

Below is a worksheet that you may find helpful. The Responsibility Worksheet is just one way to start your daughter on the path to being accountable and recognizing the consequences that come along with being a young adult. I must say that I did not design the worksheet but it has made a tremendous impact on some of the young woman that I work with. Understand that it is not about punishing our daughters for bad behavior but teaching them the hard lessons of the consequences of those behaviors.

Responsibilities: These are the things I need to take care of as a member of my family.	Privileges: These are the things that I will earn if I take care of my responsibilities.	Consequences: This is how I will lose my privileges if I don't take care of my responsibilities.
Example: Come home on time for curfew	*Go out weekdays 'til 6pm; weekends 'til 11pm*	*Not going out 1 week; early curfew 2nd week*
1)		
2)		
3)		
4)		
6)		

Tell Her to Say No to Drugs…

"Life is very interesting… in the end, some of your greatest pains, become your greatest strengths."
Drew Barrymore

For me and my family addiction has run rampant; especially for the men in my family.   More than anything I pray that my daughters will NEVER EVER give any consideration to drugs and alcohol as a way to cope with life's challenges. Drew Barrymore is best known for her role as an actress but she has successfully and gracefully overcome addiction to drugs and alcohol and is an inspiration to all who struggle with addiction.   In a telephone conversation with Drew, she said that had someone been a positive force in her life and reinforced that drug usage only leads to addiction she may not have had her public struggle with addiction. When I use the term "addiction", many of us think only in terms of a condition that involves physical dependency. This condition causes both tolerance and withdrawal, and addiction is thought to be present mainly when the withdrawal symptoms are severe. For example, long term abuse of alcohol or crystal meth can create a physical dependence that results in very serious physical withdrawal symptoms when using is stopped. But not all addiction problems create such withdrawal symptoms. Cocaine abuse or amphetamine abuse can lead to a serious addiction problem, but one that does not result in serious physical symptoms of withdrawal.

Another common misconception about addiction suggests that it occurs only when the pattern of using is severe. In truth, the extent of addiction may vary significantly, depending on the type of person and the type of substance being used. Some people naturally have a greater propensity for addictive behaviour, just as some types of substances lead more easily to addictive use. Addiction comes in various forms, from mild to severe.

Addiction primarily involves a continued desire to use a substance. The severity of an addiction problem will be determined by the extent of the use. The amount that is used, the frequency of use, and the length of time during which using has occurred all play a role in addiction. With most people and with most substances, as the amount, frequency and length of time of substance use increases, the desire to continue using will increase.

In order to avoid addiction, one might suggest that we need simply to use moderately, infrequently, or refrain from extended periods of using. This would be sound advice if not for the way our brains respond to substances. Each time we use a substance, our brains adjust to that use and then are slow to adjust back to normal, and this adjustment tends to draw us into more frequent and extensive use. A brief metaphor will help us to see this adjustment. When we first go into an air conditioned store after being outside in 95 degree heat, we very much enjoy the temperature change even though we had become accustomed to the temperature outside. Then after a while we get used to the cold air in the store, and we no longer feel it as cold. But upon returning outside, we discover that what was before more easily tolerable now feels excessively hot. We tend to want to turn around and go back inside. Use of any mood altering substance will create an adjustment in the same way. Our brain's adjustment to the presence of a substance will naturally lead to increased desires to continue using.

I don't want to go into too much detail about drug use and addiction because I think as mothers (and fathers) this is a topic that we KNOW we have to discuss with our daughters (and sons) as soon as we possibly can. I really pray that none of our daughters or sons fall victim to the perils of drugs because we all know we can lose a lot of our lives trying to figure out how to live. I hope this helps you to help your daughters understand how addiction begins so that it can be avoided in the first place. I am praying for your daughters and mine...

Tell Her to Understand Men…

"To understand how any society functions you must understand the men and women."
Angela Davis

I think it is vital that we share with our daughters the seriousness of our roles in our communities. We have already discussed the imagery that society associates with us but we haven't looked at what our role is within our society and communities. Here's some statistics to ponder.

The American Council on Education released its "Annual Status Report on Minorities in Higher Education," and it showed some disturbing trends when it comes to black males on the nation's college campuses: Their populations are not only declining, but they have the lowest graduation rate of any other group. According to the ACE report, 20 years ago, 30% of black male high school graduates were enrolled in college. It was a percentage roughly equal to the 28% for black females.

But the latest data shows that while the percentage of black male high school graduates going to college has risen to 37%, the percentage for black female high school graduates has jumped to 42%. I think more disturbing is that fact that only 35% of the black males who enter college graduate in six years. This compares to 59% for white males, 46% for Hispanic men and 45% for black females who entered college the same year. Similar studies released last year suggest that as black males drop out of college, some campuses are left with nearly twice as many black females as black males. So what does this statistical data suggest?

Well let's first understand that unlike every other race of women going to college; we have to truly be focused on getting a good education. I know we have all heard the story about finding our soul mates in college but if the statistics are as staggering as they are being reported, unless our daughters are open to inter-racial relationships they will run into dilemmas if they are looking to date African-American men exclusively.

Michelle Obama may have become an archetypal African-American female success story — law career, strong marriage, happy children — but the reality is often very different for other highly educated black women. We certainly face a series of challenges in navigating education, career, marriage and child-bearing, dilemmas that often leave us single and childless even when we would prefer marriage and family, according to a research study recently presented at the American Sociological Society's annual meeting in San Francisco.

Yale researchers Natalie Nitsche and Hannah Brueckner argued that "marriage chances for highly educated black women have declined over time relative to white women." Women of all races with postgraduate educations "face particularly hard choices between career and motherhood," they said, "but especially in the absence of a reliable partner."

A new report from Patricia Gumport, Vice Provost for graduate education at Stanford University, finds that underrepresented minorities make up 9.3% of all 8,796 graduate students at the university. Sixteen years ago in 1995, underrepresented minorities made up 10.7% of all graduate students.

The report stated that there are 279 African American graduate students at Stanford. They make up only 3.2% of all graduate students. In contrast, the latest data from the U.S. Department of Education shows that Blacks make up 7% of all undergraduate students. According to the 2011 Journal of Blacks in Higher Education (JBHE) annual survey, Blacks make up 10.7% of the entering freshman class at Stanford. This is three times the percentage of African American students in Stanford's graduate programs. The truth is the numbers for Black men and higher education is even more alarming than those already mentioned. Here are the facts surrounding educated Black women: 1) We normally put off marriage and family to complete our education and therefore, we are a little older when we set out to find true love; 2) the shortage of Black men on university campuses makes it difficult to form true relationships while obtaining higher education; and 3) most of us are unwilling to settle for a less qualified suitor for the mere fact of being "suited" with someone ~ when just anyone won't do. All this background brings me to my point: we have the task of understanding our men and trying to make sense of their absence in our lives ~ from being involved fathers to being involved mates and involved members of society.

If it is true that the women of a tribe bears the burden of mortality, then we ~ and our daughters ~ will have to acknowledge at some point that we need to build a bridge of understanding if our men are not to become obsolete. I mean the possibility is certainly there. When you remove any group from the economic structure (intentionally or otherwise), you run the risk of having the group become extinct. So when you look at the African American man being practically nonexistent on college campuses, board rooms, and in the economic structure of our society ~ what's left?

I'm telling you to make your daughters aware of the plight of African American men (and the complexities of our relationships) and allow her to determine if she wants to meet the challenge that comes along with loving Black men. She has to understand that this is a very unique challenge at best...

Tell Her to Be Her Best Invention…

Each of us has that right, that possibility, to invent ourselves daily. If a person does not invent herself, she will be invented. So to be bodacious enough to invent ourselves is wise.

Maya Angelou

Sometimes the hardest thing to do is to recognize that we can invent the person we want to become. The word "Invent" is defined as to produce (as something useful) for the first time through the use of the imagination or of ingenious thinking and experiment. We should think of ourselves as such. For was long as I can remember I have wanted to be a writer. After several foiled attempts to write a manuscript and submit to a publisher, I finally mustarded up the courage to get my thoughts on paper. Still hesitant, I let my close friends read it and repeated doubted the relevance until reluctantly submitting the finished product and having not one, but two, publishing companies stepping forward to print and distribute my first book. It was then that I became a believer in the invention process that takes place. More so it became clear that I could be anything I wanted to be.

It is vital to understand that, as I proclaim in previous chapters, our daughters have the power to be what they envision. We, as mothers, are obligated to encourage and cultivate their dreams. We, as mothers, have to further recognize that it is always easy to point out what any person is lacking but it is noble to point out those things that make our daughters unique.

My aunt once told me that, as women, we constantly have to re-invent ourselves to meet life's demands. Can't say I truly understood it at the time, but as time has passed and people have come and gone in my life, I have become a master at reinvention; reinvestment for that matter.

In doing anything of great magnitude, you first have to have the vision. Take this book for instance. I must admit it was the hardest one for me to write because I had to reach into my heart of hearts and determine the message I not only wanted ~ but needed ~ to convey within a limited amount of pages. Let's face it my books are rarely PG-13 without parental advisory and warnings; definitely not for the weak at heart or mind either. I stepped way outside of myself to invent a person who could convey a clear, concise message to mothers of teenage girls. I thought it was certainly a message that needed to be promoted because of the number of teenage girls and young women that I personally run into that lack the guidance of a mother-figure. For some people that's hard to imagine so let me share the statistics.

1. There are approximately 1.7 million homeless teens in the U.S.

2. 39 percent of the homeless population is young people under 18.

3. About 75 percent of homeless teens use drugs or alcohol as a means to self-medicate to deal with the traumatic experiences and abuse they face.

4. 5,000 young people die every year because of assault, illness, or suicide while on the street.

5. A U.S. Department of Health and Human Services study found that 46 percent of homeless youth left their home because of physical abuse. 17 percent left because of sexual abuse.

6. Approximately 40 percent of homeless teens identify as LGBT.

7. Over 50 percent of young people in shelters and on the streets report that their parents told them to leave or knew they were leaving and didn't care.

8. The average age a teen becomes homeless is 14.7 years.

9. 1 in 7 young people between the ages of 10 and 18 will run away.

10. Teens age 12 to 17 are more likely to become homeless than adults.

11. HIV rates for homeless young people are 2 to 10 times higher than reported rates for other samples of adolescents in the U.S.

In one study, almost half of the youth interviewed said parent/guardian conflicts were a problem before they left home and landed in a runaway or homeless youth shelter. Another study, conducted with shelter personnel, suggested that a problematic relationship with a parent or another adult at home led to running away 75 percent of the time. In 2011, 28 percent of crisis callers to National Runaway Switchboard identified family dynamics as a problem for them. The most common reason for running away from home given by a non-random sample of youth who are lesbian, gay, bisexual or transgender (LGBT) is rejection by family of the youth's sexual orientation or gender identity (46%). In addition, 42 percent of LGBT youth report being forced out of their homes by their parents.

I'm the first one to admit that I can be very tough on my daughters because I expect so much from them. And I use to feel like, with all the compromises I have made to raise them properly, the very least thing they can do was be successful at EVERYTHING. How unrealistic was that?

...And it doesn't stop there! To the mothers, we got some work to do to ~ all change begins with us. We have to own it!

Change means reinvention. Each time a major shift happens in our lives—leaving a job or a relationship, moving, losing a loved one—we have to take control of who we will become or risk never reaching our full potential. I've reinvented myself several times in my life. Most adults have.

But what I always forget is that we have to choose reinvention. Each time I've done it, I've forged my new path deliberately and with foresight.

When I've waited for my future to find me, I've waited in vain, lost in confusion and sadness, or I've gotten tangled up in a situation I didn't want.

One morning, after struggling for months with grief and loss, I woke up and realized that I was having so much trouble moving forward partly because I had no idea what it was that I wanted to move towards. I was thinking about my past, but not what I wanted for my future.

That morning, I woke with a vision: a crowd of people from the life I needed to leave behind with the sun rising opposite them and me standing between the two, the sun beating down on my face. In the vision, I decided, finally, to turn from the group and walk towards the sun, my new life.

That vision told me what I needed to hear—that I had to take control of my future instead of letting my pain choose for me.

These are 5 steps I've identified to reinvent yourself:

1. Create a vision for your future.

Sit quietly, close your eyes, and imagine the people, places, or situations that you need to leave behind. Now imagine the future that you want, whether it's simply a feeling, a group of people, or a situation such as a wonderful new job.

Imagine how it will feel to be in that new place. Picture the sun coming up behind your future, the warm glow of the light on your face.

Stand for a moment and silently voice your appreciation of everything that came before. Once you've thanked the past, turn toward the sun, and with compassion and gratitude, imagine yourself walking away from the past and into the future.

2. Write about your reinvention.

Imagine a scene from it or write about how you'd like it to play out. Where are you living? What do you do in the mornings, afternoon, evenings? Who are your friends? What do you spend your days doing?

Continue writing for as long as this exercise feels invigorating and exciting. Write scenes, dialogues, lists, plans. Make the future come alive. Write about how it will feel to be there. Keep your writing somewhere where you will look at it occasionally. Feel free to add to it.

3. Surround yourself with visual reminders of the life you'd like to create.

If it's a new job in a particular field, put objects or images from that field someplace where you'll see them every day. If it's a home, find a picture of a house that you love and put it near your front door. It can be anything that reminds you of what you're moving toward.

4. Now that you have a vision of your future, break it up into workable tasks.

What do you need to do—every day—to create that vision? Look for work? Meet new people? Search for a place to live in your chosen town? Make it specific. Make a list of everything you need to do and a schedule for when you'll do it. Then do it and commit to keep doing it, one day at a time.

5. Every day, go back to that vision of you walking towards your future.

Every morning or evening, close your eyes, and see yourself walking into the rising sun, toward your dreams, and reconnect with why you're moving toward this new possibility.

Reinvention is neither easy nor always smooth. Often we encounter resistance. We don't want to let go, even of things that cause us pain or that are obviously already out of our grasp. We often struggle with limiting beliefs or stories about ourselves that hold us back from trying new things.

But there is one way to keep your compass pointed to this new life, even in the midst of any resistance or struggles you may encounter on your path.

Each time you find yourself slipping into old habits—isolating yourself, making excuses not to look for work, procrastinating on a task that might help you advance in your career—don't bother wondering why you're doing it or beating yourself up.

Just ask yourself this: "What can I do in this moment to keep moving forward?"

Then, no matter what you feel in the moment—lonely, self-critical, tired, lazy, or disappointed—do something to maintain momentum, even if it's one small thing. There's an old adage that says that true courage isn't about not feeling fear; it's about feeling fear and acting anyway.

Have the courage to choose instead of letting your fear choose for you...

Tell her to put God first…

Many people miss out on living the "blessed life" because they fail to put God first. How about you? Is God first in your life?

"First's" are important to God. Remember, in the First Commandment, God said, "You shall have no other gods before me" (Exodus 20:3). Put simply, He wants to be first in everything.

In order for your life to be blessed, God must come first. He wants you to put Him before your church, your job, your money, your "things," even your spouse and children. He wants to be your number one priority.

Not putting God first is like buttoning your coat incorrectly. If you get the first button wrong, all the others will be wrong. But when you get the first button right, all the others will line up. When you put God first, everything else in your life will line up, too.

First Things First...
God has a wonderful benefits package prepared for all who will put Him first. It is designed to cover all of our daily needs and keep us free from anxiety, as Jesus described in Matthew 6:25-33:

"Therefore I say to you, do not worry about your life, what you will eat or what you will drink; nor about your body, what you will put on. Is not life more than food and the body more than clothing? Look at the birds of the air, for they neither sow nor reap nor gather into barns; yet your heavenly Father feeds them. Are you not of more value than they? Which of you by worrying can add one cubit to his stature?

"So why do you worry about clothing? Consider the lilies of the field, how they grow: they neither toil nor spin; and yet I say to you that even Solomon in all his glory was not arrayed like one of these. Now if God so clothes the grass of the field, which today is, and tomorrow is thrown into the oven, will He not much more clothe you, O you of little faith?

"Therefore do not worry, saying, 'What shall we eat?' or 'What shall we drink?' or 'What shall we wear?' For after all these things the Gentiles seek. For your heavenly Father knows that you need all these things. But seek first the kingdom of God and His righteousness, and all these things shall be added to you."

Jesus isn't saying that it's wrong to work for food, shelter and clothing; He just wants us to keep our priorities straight. He wants our hearts to be set on the spiritual (eternal) rather than on the physical (temporary). When we put His kingdom and eternal things first, God assures us that we will have the other things that we need.

Time, Treasure and Talents ...

Everything we have comes from God. He created the heavens and the earth. He made us and breathed life into our lungs. He gave each of us time, treasure and talents to use while living on earth, and He will bless whatever we dedicate to Him.

The devil, however, does not want you to experience a blessed life. In fact, John 10:10 tells us that the devil comes to steal, kill, and destroy. He will try to do whatever he can to keep you from using your time, treasures and talents first and foremost for God. But Jesus said, "I have come that they may have life, and that they may have it more abundantly." If you and I truly want to live blessed lives, the devil cannot stop us!

It's important for each of us to evaluate our priorities from time to time to avoid being distracted from putting God first. If you are not seeing God's blessing in action, then it is especially important to consider what you are doing with your time, treasure and talents. If you are already putting God first, then let this article simply be an encouragement to keep it up!

Time

God created everything – even time. Solomon, the wisest man who ever lived, made it very clear in Ecclesiastes that, from being born to dying, there is a time for everything.

The Apostle Paul wrote about our use of time in Ephesians 5:15-17. He said, "Look carefully then how you walk! Live purposefully and worthily and accurately, not as the unwise and witless, but as wise (sensible, intelligent people), making the very most of the time [buying up each opportunity], because the days are evil. Therefore, do not be vague and thoughtless and foolish, but understanding and firmly grasping what the will of the Lord is" (Amplified).

When was the last time you stopped and reflected on how you are using your time – the time God has given you? Think about it: are you putting God first with your time by spending it on things that honor Him? For example, do you dedicate time each day to scripture reading and prayer, or do you watch your favorite TV programs instead? Do you spend "quality" time with your spouse and children, encouraging them in the Lord? Do you spend more time talking about weather and sports or talking about what Jesus has done for you?

Treasure

The Bible has a lot to say about money and material possessions. Sixteen of Jesus' parables (and one out of every ten New Testament verses) deal with money, so it is apparent that how we feel about money - and what we do with it - is important to God.

Jesus said, "Do not lay up for yourselves treasures on earth, where moth and rust destroy and where thieves break in and steal; but lay up for yourselves treasures in heaven, where neither moth nor rust destroys and where thieves do not break in and steal. For where your treasure is, there your heart will be also" (Matthew 6:19-21). Earthly treasures are temporary, but the money you spend on eternal things like preaching the gospel, giving to help people, etc. makes an impact that will last forever!

Think about how you use the money God has entrusted you with. Are you faithful in giving God the first ten percent? Are you using a portion of it to take good care of your family? Do you show your thanks to God by giving cheerfully and generously to the things that are on His heart, or do you give Him what is left over after most of your money is spent?

The Israelites dedicated the first and the best of their produce, cattle, birds, etc. to the Lord and then lived on the rest. Are you giving God your "first fruits" or your "last fruits"?

Talents

1 Corinthians 12:18 tells us that, "God has set the members, each one of them, in the body just as He pleased." He has given every person talents and abilities that should be used to honor Him and be a blessing to others.

Too often, people use their talents only for their own personal gratification, to make a living, or to impress others. It is good to ask yourself, "Am I using my talents for the Lord? Am I doing what God wants me to do? Am I making a difference in the kingdom of God?"

Remember, life on earth is temporary. God has given us all we are and all we have—our time, treasure and talents - to invest for His kingdom and glory. As you "seek first the kingdom of God" with your time, your treasure and your talents, you will experience the blessed life God has planned for you. You'll see His power actively working in you, through you, and for you. His blessing will affect every area of your life including your marriage, your family, your relationships, your health, and your finances.

That's the kind of life you can have when you put God first.

(All scriptures are from the New King James Version of the Bible unless otherwise stated.)

A Message from the Author...

I Am...

A sinner saved by grace... now a redeemed, a priest, a queen... a learning lover, poet and warrior... a grateful inspiration and hopeful blessing... Wonderfully Made, Faithfully Minded, Amazingly Redeemed, Caringly Nurtured, Truly Blessed, Highly Favored and Deeply Loved!

For surely, O Lord, you bless the righteous. I, therefore, declare that I am blessed through Jesus Christ. Thank You for surrounding me with Your favor as with a shield. I thank You, Lord, that I can abound in your favor and blessing today. I, therefore, expect Your favor to go before me today. I anticipate the favor of God surrounding me and I expect my Heavenly Father to give me favor with men, even with the ungodly.

I thank You Heavenly Father for opening doors for me that neither man nor the devil can shut. Thank You for blessing the works of my hands as I walk under an open heaven. May I experience your supernatural increase and provision in every area of my life this day. I choose to walk in faith and in victory.

In Jesus' name I pray.
Amen.

4363528R00037

Printed in Great Britain
by Amazon.co.uk, Ltd.,
Marston Gate.